The Tree in the Moon

and other legends of plants and trees

by Rosalind Kerven

illustrated by Bryna Waldman

CAMBRIDGE UNIVERSITY PRESS

Cambridge

New York   Port Chester

Melbourne   Sydney

Other legends books from Cambridge

Legends of Journeys by Olga Norris

Legends of the Animal World by Rosalind Kerven

Legends of Earth, Air, Fire and Water by Eric and Tessa Hadley

Legends of the Sun and Moon by Eric and Tessa Hadley

The Seven Wonders of the World by Kenneth McLeish

The Shining Stars by Ghislaine Vautier and Kenneth McLeish

The Way of the Stars by Ghislaine Vautier and Kenneth McLeish

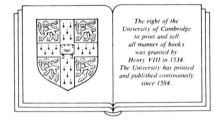
Published by the Press Syndicate of the University of Cambridge
The Pitt Building, Trumpington Street, Cambridge CB2 1RP
32 East 57th Street, New York, NY 10022, USA
10 Stamford Road, Oakleigh, Melbourne 3166, Australia

First published 1989

Printed in Hong Kong by Wing King Tong

British Library cataloguing in publication data
Kerven, Rosalind
    The tree in the moon and other legends of plants and trees.
    I. Title   II. Waldman, Bryna
    823′.914 [J]   PZ7

Library of Congress cataloging in publication data
Kerven, Rosalind.
    The tree in the moon and other legends of plants and trees.
    Summary: A collection of traditional tales about plants and
trees from a variety of cultures.
    1. Plants – Folklore – Juvenile literature.
2. Trees – Folklore – Juvenile literature. 3. Tales
[1. Plants – Folklore. 2. Trees – Folklore. 3. Folklore]
I. Waldman, Bryna, ill. II. Title.
PZ8.1.K45Tr   1988   398.2′42   87-21858

ISBN 0 521 34269 4

DS

CONTENTS

THE TREE IN THE MOON

Come . . .

Back through time to the day when Hina the goddess and her brother Ru sailed the shimmering seas.

They were mighty explorers! They knew every corner of the ocean, every reef, every current, every quirk of the waves, like their own hands.

Hina was brave and insatiabl[y] curious: she longed to find somewhere new, beyond the oceans of Earth, somewhere reall[y] different . . .

'I want to go to the Moon,' s[he] said.

She went alone, sailing her canoe far, far out through the Sky into the deep, empty stillness of Space.

The Moon lit her way like a brilliantly flaming torch, swirling with dark, mysterious shadows. Hina could not take her eyes off i[t]

Closer and closer she drifted. At last she could see the shadows quite clearly. They were the roots and branches of a *tree*!

Yes, the whole Moon was covered by a single, enormous banyan tree. It had hundreds of trunks, each one as thick and gnarled as a huddle of old men. Its thousands of roots were like a coarse tangle of fishing nets. When the lonely winds of outer space blew, a million-million leaves rustled and sighed.

Hina's boat came to rest in that secret place where the Moon's bright side melts into the dark. She moored it carefully, jumped out and began to wander through this strange and wonderful new land.

She found that the tree had grown into a network of tunnels, caverns and clearings, lit by pale blue, dappled Earthlight. It smelt of dew and new leaves and – something sweet . . .

Mmmm! Thick bunches of red figs, dripping with juice, were dangling from the topmost branches.

Hina's mouth watered. She stood on tiptoe and tried to reach them . . .

'*U'upa!*'

A loud squawk made her jump out of her skin. The biggest fig she had ever seen landed at her feet – followed by a beautiful, glossy green parrot.

'Hello friend,' laughed Hina when she had got over her surprise. 'What a lovely world this Moon is! You know, I've sailed beyond the edges of everywhere in my life, but I've never found a place I liked as much. I think I shall stay here for ever.'

So Hina built a little tree house and settled down. To amuse herself, she took to stripping bark from the banyan and beating it into beautiful *tapa*-cloth, tinted with moonbeams.

With U'upa the parrot chattering away all day, she was never lonely. Yet sometimes when she gazed at the blue, far away Earth, she would feel a pang of homesickness.

'How can I be sure that my people down there won't forget me?' she sighed. 'I know! I shall send them down some gifts from this marvellous tree.'

So she plucked a handful of figs and gave them to U'upa. The parrot flew with them as far as he dared into the dark, lonely fringes of space. Then he opened his beak and flung them with all his might,

down . . .

down . . .

hurtling towards Earth . . .

Many times the tides rose and fell, many times the stars traced their paths across the sky.

The figs landed safely. They sank roots into the soil. They sent up shoots. They grew – into the very first banyan trees in all the world!

To this day they're still growing, fine and strong, in memory of the goddess Hina.

As for Hina herself – if you're sharp-eyed when the Moon is full, you can still see her up there quite clearly, clambering happily about in the Moon Tree's shadowy branches.

Tahitian

IMPRISONED IN A TREE!

Beware the forest! Beware the *ngarri*!

Oh, you young daredevils: let this story be a warning – never ever venture through the bush on your own . . .

There were once two boys who went out gathering honey. Along the track of the wild bees they wandered, laughing, joking, high up in the hollow trees, deep in the heart of the forest.

They were just shinning down from some of the highest, honey-rich branches, when suddenly they saw a white, dazzling . . . *something* lurking at the foot of the tree.

The two friends clung to the tree trunk, frozen with fear. It was a *ngarri*, an evil forest spirit!

There was no escape.

The brightness was coiled hugely, tightly round the roots. As they watched, slowly it seemed to change, like the curling of fire-smoke; until it transformed itself into an enormous, hideously ugly woman.

'Got you!' she shrieked.

With a scrawny, warty hand she plucked the boys from the tree trunk and stuffed them into a big pot which she carried under her arm.

'Help, help!' yelled the boys; but no-one heard them.

The *ngarri* began to run through the forest. Inside her pot, the boys bumped and thumped painfully along, until at last she stopped in front of another tree.

This tree was so tall that its branches almost touched the sky. Through the narrow opening of the pot, they saw the *ngarri* peel back a piece of its bark like a door.

A strange, sad sound drifted out, like the shadows of many voices whimpering.

The next thing they knew, the boys were being tossed out of the pot and tumbling into the pitch-black depths of the hollow tree.

The bark door slammed tightly shut behind them.

'Help, help!' they yelled again.

A hundred shadow-voices sighed from the darkness: 'Don't waste your breath, for no-one will ever hear you and everything is hopeless.'

'Who's there?' whispered the friends.

'Once we were boys like you,' said the voices, 'but we have wasted away into spirits. The wicked *ngarri* is fattening us up. Very soon she is going to eat us!'

It was quite true. Every day, the *ngarri* went hunting, and every night she pushed armfuls of meat into the hollow for the captured boys to eat.

There was nothing to do inside the tree except to eat, to wait and to be afraid. In this way, the two boys quickly grew so fat that soon it was almost their turn to be gobbled up.

'We must get out of this tree before it's too late,' declared the first boy.

'But how?' said his friend. 'We haven't got any tools or weapons.'

'You're wrong! I've been thinking: we have our nose-bones. Listen, this is my plan . . .'

Very carefully, the boys removed the sharp, hollow bones

that they wore as ornaments in their noses. They pressed them against the bark-door. Then they blew down them – *huff – puff – huff*! with all their might until suddenly – *wooosh*! – the bark fell away and they tumbled right out of the tree!

Oh, then you can be sure that they ran like the wind – through the trees, out of the forest, back, back, safely to their camp . . .

The boys lived on and grew into mighty hunters. The story of their terrible adventure became famous around the evening fires.

They are long fallen now. The old trees have fallen too, and new ones grow tall and broad in their place. Yet, still sometimes strange noises float from the forest like the cries of lost children. And when the sunlight flickers and dazzles through distant roots and branches – who knows? Can it be that the evil old *ngarri* is on the prowl again?

Aboriginal

TREES OF FIRE

Many, many seasons ago, before there were any people, the world was ruled by animals and trees. At that time, only the Pine Trees knew about fire. They guarded their knowledge selfishly, for it was a treasure that set them above the rest.

It was winter. Thick snow lay everywhere. The rivers froze, the dew froze, even the air was thick with ice.

Most of the trees were still and silent. All the animals shivered and huddled together. 'Oh, oh, we're freezing to death!' Their frightened whispers were like icicles in the wind.

But down on the river bank, the Pines were having a party, with an enormous fire burning to keep themselves warm.

Beaver saw them. He was so angry that he plunged straight through the ice into the river and swam to the bank where the Pines' fire was blazing.

There he hid, watched, waited . . .

Suddenly, a burning coal rolled out of the fire and came tumbling towards him in a red–hot ball of flame.

Beaver darted out and snatched the coal. Clasping it tight against his fur, he dived back deep into the water, sending up a hissing jet of steam.

'*STOP*!' roared the Pines with one voice. There was a horrible tearing noise as they heaved and wrenched their roots out from the frosty ground – *aaargh*! *umff*! *blump*! – and then they began to run.

They lumbered along, dark and heavy over the snow and ice, with their needles showering down in green, prickly splutters of anger.

'Thief! Fire is *our* secret!'

But Beaver just carried on swimming swiftly down the river, chuckling and chattering over his precious coal.

Day darkened into night. Still the army of Pines chased Beaver;

but now the trees were tiring. They were not used to running. Their roots were cracked and broken.

A groan ran through them. They panted and swayed into a thicket; their branches tangled painfully; they tripped and twisted over their own roots; finally they stopped.

Beaver stopped too and looked around.

He was no longer being chased. Instead, all the Pines stood stock still, rooted into a dark,

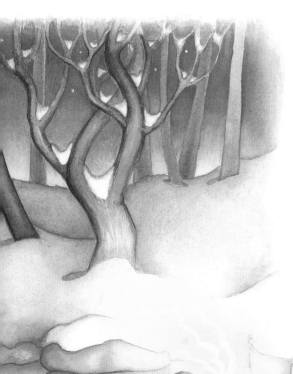

brooding forest. He was safe!

The little animal drifted on down the river. What should he do with his treasure now? If only he could make its flame grow to warm the chill of winter . . . He rubbed the smouldering coal thoughtfully. '*Ow!*' The fire leaped out and burned his paws.

'Fire is too dangerous for me,' he sighed.

Presently, on the opposite bank of the river, he spied another clump of trees with bare, thin branches patiently suffering the cold.

'Good news, friends!' he called to them. 'I have found fire! But I don't know what to do with it. Can *you* take care of it? Would you share its warmth with all who need it?'

A breeze stirred.

'Yes, yes,' the slender Willows nodded shyly back at him.

'Oh *yes*,' echoed the gentle Birches.

So Beaver crossed the river and passed fire into the Willows and Birches.

At once its magic flashed through their sap. They rubbed

their twigs together: flames danced out, bright and welcoming as the sun!

Since that day, the Willows and Birches have guarded fire well and generously. Seek them out if ever you are cold in the wilderness. Break their twigs carefully, rub them together in the time-honoured way. If you are a friend to all that breathe and grow, the trees will gladly share fire with you.

Nez Percé Indian

THE MYSTERY MAN OF THE PEONIES

Princess Aya was engaged to be married!

Everyone in the Palace of Adzuchi-no-Shiro was wild with excitement at the news – everyone, that is, except for Princess Aya herself.

For *she* had never even met the man who was soon to be her husband. Her father, Lord Yuki, had arranged it all privately with the bridegroom's father, and Aya was told she had better agree to the wedding, or else . . . !

Supposing he was ugly or stupid or cruel? Supposing she just didn't *like* him?

All day, Aya sat brooding and worrying. At last she could bear it no longer. Calling to her maids to follow, she went out into the cool air of the palace gardens.

The day had already wasted away into darkness, but the moon was silvery bright.

She went straight down to the lake and gazed mournfully across the rippling water. The maids waited a respectful distance behind.

All of a sudden, Aya screamed.

On the muddy shore, her foot slipped: she grabbed wildly at a tree, a bush – but it was no use. Down and away she went, tumbling rapidly towards the deep, dark lake!

At once, the maids rushed to save her; but in that very instant they were stopped in their tracks by an extraordinary, dazzling flash of light.

'Princess! Are you all right?'

There was no answer.

Then, just as quickly, the light faded and – oh, relief! – there she was, standing safely on the bank. Yet strangely, her tears were all gone, and now a radiant smile lit her face.

The maids stared at her in bewilderment. At last one plucked up enough courage to ask,

'Your Highness – what are you smiling at? And what on earth happened to you just now?'

Aya turned round slowly. She looked dazed.

'Oh, he was so kind and handsome!' she whispered. 'If only *he* were to be my husband!'

'Whoever are you talking about, Princess?'

'That man who leapt out from the peony bushes just now,' said Aya. 'He saved me from falling into the water! Oh, whoever can he be? And where has he disappeared to?'

'I didn't see anyone,' said the maid. 'Did you?'

The others solemnly shook their heads.

'But you *must* have done!' cried Aya. 'He was so finely dressed! His clothes were embroidered all over with peonies – as if he knew that they're my favourite flower!'

'You had better not let your father hear about this, your Highness,' the maid said gently. 'You know what he does to trespassers. He'll get the guards to chop this man's head off if he ever finds out!'

'Heaven forbid!' exclaimed Aya. And she swore her maids to secrecy.

Many days passed and the wedding drew nearer; but Aya went down with a mysterious illness which forced it to be delayed. She grew pale and listless. At night she lay awake weeping. By day she had no zest for anything, but to walk round and round by the same bed of peonies that grew by the water's edge.

In truth, she was sick with love.

'What's this all about?' demanded Lord Yuki at last. He was impatient to see his daughter married off as quickly as possible.

He called her terrified maids into his presence under armed guard, and forced them to confess everything they knew.

★

That night the palace grounds were all a-buzz with merriment. Lord Yuki had arranged for a concert on the terrace above the garden, 'To shake the girl out of her ridiculous melancholy.'

As darkness fell, the musicians came out with their instruments. At the same time, strong shadows moved silently among the bushes, for his lordship had sent soldiers swarming everywhere to catch and execute the intruder.

At first, Aya listened to the music as stiffly and blankly as a statue. Then suddenly she gave a strangled cry:

'There! Oh my love!'

She stood up and began to run down the terrace steps, as if drawn on a string towards the peony bushes.

Every eye turned. There was that strange, flickering light again –

but this time everyone could see through it quite clearly.

A young man stood there. He was handsome and gallant indeed, with his fine, silken robes embroidered with Aya's favourite peonies.

'Seize him!' roared Lord Yuki. At once three officers rushed forward, swords held high and . . .

. . . And stopped in mid-air – for in that instant, the young man disappeared!

He was gone, utterly, absolutely not there.

All that night and the next day, Lord Yuki's anger flared and smouldered; and the terrible, lovesick aching burned through Aya's heart.

She *must* find him, talk with him, beg him to take her away . . . Oh, if only he could!

The next night they held another concert.

This time, barely five minutes had passed before Princess Aya was gasping, rising to her feet and racing towards the handsome young man who appeared yet again in the peonies.

'*Stop them!*' The words had scarcely left Lord Yuki's lips before Princess Aya was grabbed by two of his guards . . . and then, oh horror! – her beloved stranger was a prisoner too with a dagger gleaming at his throat!

Then there was utter confusion. Light flashed blindingly, the guards staggered, voices shouted and screamed. Slowly, slowly, the light crumbled into a wet, shimmering mist . . .

Lord Yuki strode forward, pushing the mist aside like a curtain. There before him stood the two soldiers who had pounced on the stranger. One still held his dagger – pointed at thin, empty air. The other was gazing foolishly down at his own muscley arms, which were clasped around – not the young man – but a single peony flower!

'My lord,' he murmured humbly, 'I . . . um . . . the villain seems to have . . . er . . . got away.'

He met Lord Yuki's thunderous look, and glanced down again at the flower.

'He . . . um . . . seems to have left this.'

'This *flower*?' said Lord Yuki.

The soldier nodded humbly. But to his surprise, Lord Yuki's tone suddenly changed.

'Ah,' he said softly, 'I believe I understand. Some miracle has taken place before our very eyes. The stranger who stole my daughter's heart must be the spirit of these peony bushes that made itself into human shape! I have heard of such magic, but to think that it should happen here, to us . . . !'

He took the flower from the soldier and gave it to his trembling daughter.

'Here,' he said gruffly, 'You may keep this. It will be harmless now.' He coughed. 'I know how you love peonies.'

Princess Aya took the flower to her room. She stood it in a vase of water on a little table beside her bed.

After that, her dreams each night were sweetened by its perfume. Her heart lightened and all her cares fell away as if her true love dwelt beside her.

Day by day, her health improved. And day by day, the flower bloomed and showed no sign of fading.

But now that Princess Aya was well again, there was no longer any reason to delay her wedding. So before the next moon was full in the sky, the unlucky girl was married.

On the very day of her wedding, at the very hour, the wondrous peony flower suddenly wilted and died.

Japanese

GRANNY AND THE ELDER TREE WITCH

Did you know that a witch can turn herself into an elder tree?

No? Well, Farmer Brown didn't believe it either – until the day he discovered someone had been stealing his milk.

The thief had sneaked out during the darkest, spookiest hours of night and had milked his cows quite dry!

Well, the farmer thought himself a brave enough man, so the next night he sat up under the stars, shivering and watching his herd; and what should he see but the shadow of a *tree* with a milk-churn in its branches, moving in and out amongst the cows.

All in a hot and cold sweat he hurried home, and not a wink did he sleep that night.

Next morning he told his womenfolk all about it.

His wife banged the pan of porridge down.

'Nonsense!' she scolded, 'you're going soft in the head, man!'

His daughter peeped through the window and turned as pale as curd-cheese.

'Nonsense it isn't,' she screamed, 'for I can see the tree in the field now. Ooooh! It's marching after all the cows!'

Then old Granny heaved herself up, shuffling over to stoke the fire with a massive iron poker.

'Nonsense we won't have,' she muttered. 'An elder tree, is it? Then it will be *my* pleasure to make an end of it!'

'Pshaw!' grunted the farmer. 'It needs a *man* to deal with a fiend like this.' With that, he loaded his gun and strode with it boldly out through the door.

But as soon as he got within shooting range of the Elder Tree Witch, he began to shudder and tremble, *ugg-ga-ga-ga!* from his head down to his boots. He took aim and pulled the trigger; but his hand was so wobbly that the shot missed the tree completely and went whizzing over the head of his cows.

The poor beasts scattered everywhere. What a panic and commotion! Out of the thick of it all came the Elder Tree Witch with a whoosh and a cackle and a shriek, racing towards him and rattling her branches. Farmer Brown whirled round and fairly pelted back to the house – and all the time, the tree was chasing after him like mad.

With not a second to spare, he made it inside, slammed the door shut and slid the bolt firmly to.

From outside came a horrible moaning like a high wind battering the chimneys. The door began to shake, and the shuttered windows to rat-a-tat-tattle, as the witch's raggedy branches scratched and tore to break in.

Farmer Brown just stood there, paralysed with fear, and so did his wife and daughter; but old Granny chuckled calmly and carried the shovel to her blazing fire.

Umph! With one stroke of her scrawny arm she had it full of blazing coals.

'Open the door!' she yelled at her granddaughter.

The poor, terrified girl heaved back the bolt and flung the door open. The Elder Tree Witch was waiting right outside!

Granny took a good, long look at the evil one. Then she flung her shovel of coals, *smack!* right at the elder tree's branches.

There was a gigantic, blinding flash – then the tree burst into a dazzling frenzy of blue flames. And soon nothing was left of it but a crackling heap of evil smelling cinders.

Not long after this happened, news reached the Browns about crotchetty old Raggy Lyddy, who used to live in the lonely hovel down by the mill. That very same morning, it seemed, she had fallen asleep into her fire and got herself burned to death.

'Ah,' said Granny knowingly, 'So that's the one who turned into a tree – she was the witch that I burned!'

English

THE KING AND THE THORN TREE BRIDE

Back in the days before our great-great-grandfathers were young, the medicine men discovered how to turn trees into women. Yes, it's true! In fact, the magic was so easy that, with a little practice, any man could do it for himself. However, it didn't always work out too well, as a fellow called Yo found out.

One day this Yo was out gathering firewood when he stumbled upon a thorn-tree. It was covered all over in fragrant white blossom, and he thought to himself, *If I had a wife as pretty and sweet as this, never mind her prickly thorns, how happy I would be!*

So he strutted up to the tree, put an arm around its trunk and whispered enticingly, 'Hey beautiful, if you turn yourself into a lady, I'll marry you at once and give you everything your heart desires!'

Well, the thorn tree waved her branches about coyly and answered through a rustle of leaves, 'Yes Yo, I'll do it! But first you must make me a promise: you must never accuse me of being a tree instead of a real woman.'

'Me do such a thing?' cried Yo, 'Never!'

'That's good,' said the thorn tree. 'Well then, turn your back and don't look until I say.'

So Yo turned round, almost jumping up and down with excitement. After a few moments she called, 'You can look now.'

And when he did, oh my, she was every bit as lovely as he had hoped!

'You can call me Yawo,' she told him.

As Yo led her home, the whole forest seemed perfumed with her blossom. They set up house together as husband and wife and Yo was blissfully happy. It never crossed his mind that his lovely Yawo might be making someone very jealous.

Oho! And who was the owner of the jealous heart? It was none other than the king himself!

When King Dada Segbo saw Yo and Yawo walking hand in hand through the forest, he couldn't get over her beauty.

'What a woman!' he exclaimed. 'She's much too fine for a fat, greedy wretch like Yo. She ought to be *my* wife!'

Well, a king can usually get what he wants without too much trouble.

One day Yo went out to work in his fields as usual, and when he got back he found the whole village milling around outside his house in great excitement.

'Yo, Yo,' shouted his neighbours, 'your beloved Yawo has gone! The king's soldiers called while you were out. They took her prisoner and led her away!'

Yo stomped angrily into his house and found that what they said was indeed true. Oh, his heart felt as heavy as a lump of stone. But out of his anger grew cunning. For many hours he sat alone indoors brooding; until at last he hatched a plan.

Next morning he dressed in his finest clothes and paid a visit to the royal palace of Dada Segbo.

He found the king seated in state. His carved throne was inlaid with gold and silver, plumped with scarlet and emerald silken cushions, cooled by slaves with horsetail fans.

'What do you want of me, worm?' he demanded.

'Great majesty,' said Yo, 'you have stolen my wife. What an honour that is for a humble man like myself! I have come to say thank you.'

The king grinned nastily.

'You had better thank me well,' he said. 'I have no time for half-wits. What will you do for me?'

'If you will let me, I would like to come and play my drum for you', said Yo. 'Though I say it myself, I'm the best drummer for miles around, your majesty. When you hear me play, I promise your whole court will want to get up and dance.'

'That pleases me,' nodded the king. 'I like dancing. You may come back and entertain me in three days' time.'

So at the appointed hour, Yo returned to the palace. Small as an

ant under the towering, painted walls of the courtyard, he settled down with his drum and began to play.

By and by the king came out followed by a long procession of all his wives. They swayed their hips as they caught the rhythm of Yo's music – fifty, one-hundred, three-hundred queens! – and right at the back came Yawo, the lovely thorn tree bride.

When he saw her, Yo's hands pounded across his drum skin fast and light as rain beating on the high roof of the forest.

King Dada Segbo smiled, nodded and began to dance. The three hundred queens danced too, bending and whirling in perfect harmony to Yo's fine, pattering music. Then one by one they tired and sank to the floor to rest around the king, until only Yawo was left dancing.

O-o-oh! When she twirled her hands it was like leaves fluttering in the breeze that comes with the cool of evening. A-a-ah! Her arms and legs were like dark, slender branches. Everywhere the thick scent of thorn blossom followed her through the air.

Yo drummed harder, faster, better than he had ever done before. He watched Yawo through narrowed eyes until at last his anger boiled over and he began to sing:

Oh lovely Yawo!
Once you were humble Yo's bride
But now you are married to a king.

Oh mighty Dada Segbo,
You have stolen a poor man's wife –
Now you shall feel the sting!

Oh all who listen,
Hear the truth: Yawo is no woman
But a thorn tree that I found! . . .

Yawo stopped dancing. She turned, glared at Yo and shrieked at him, 'You've broken your promise! You swore you'd never blame me for being a tree before I was a woman!'

But Yo was so angry he just carried on drumming and singing:

'Oh yes, I'll kill the magic!
Yawo is just a rotten old tree,
A prickly lump of wood torn up from
*   the ground!'*

Now King Dada Segbo's eye glowered dangerously; then suddenly he threw up his arms and roared, 'My little queen is fleeing! Catch her – or I'll chop off all your heads!'

For Yawo was no longer dancing but running – bursting out through the passages of the palace. At once the royal soldiers dashed forward; Yawo quickened her pace, swift as a hunted gazelle.

But the soldiers gained on her – faster – faster – caught her – touched her – seized her roughly by the arm – and Yawo ran no more. She could not run. She was no longer a woman . . .

For the king had done wrong: he should not have stolen a poor man's wife. Yo had done wrong too: he should not have broken his promise and broken the magic.

That is why Yawo was rooted to the ground again. She was not made for arguments, tricks or treachery; so she turned back into a tree.

Dahomean (West African)

THE GOOD SISTER AND THE MANGO TREE

When Kapil was a lad, he always said that his best friend was his little sister, Sumitra. Honestly, the things they got up to together! Soon enough they grew up,

Kapil got married and set up house with his new wife, Bindu; and Sumitra went to live with them.

Now Bindu did not like this at all. In her eyes, Sumitra was just a clinging, lazy nuisance.

'What does she do all day?' she complained. 'Nothing, I tell you, *nothing*!'

'That's not true,' replied Kapil gently. 'She looks after the garden beautifully – especially my favourite mango tree.

'Oh that silly tree! Every time I go outside she's drooling over it with her watering pot. She even *talks* to it!'

Kapil grinned and said nothing.

'Very funny!' Bindu shrieked, 'but who's left to do all the work? Who has to fetch the water, light the fire, do all the cooking – *and* wash the dishes afterwards? It's me, me, *me*!'

'Indeed, you work very hard,' Kapil agreed. 'Thank you – you're a wonderful wife.'

Bindu sniffed. 'Hmph! The point is, what's going to become of *her*? It's high time she was married.

Now, Kapil had to admit that people were beginning to whisper about Sumitra being 'left on the shelf'. So as was the custom, he set out to make enquiries in search of a nice man who would make his dear sister happy.

Before long, he had introduced Sumitra to a suitable bridegroom.

All through the wedding, Bindu was beaming with joy. At last it was time for Sumitra to leave with her new husband.

'Goodbye sister-in-law,' she said to Bindu. 'Look after my brother, won't you? Oh, and please, *please* take good care of my special little mango tree.'

Bindu smiled pleasantly; but secretly she thought, *What a cheek*!

After the wedding she was much happier now that she had Kapil all to herself. As for the mango tree – she made a special point of neglecting it.

She did not water it and she she did not weed it. Before long, the poor tree began to wilt and lose its leaves.

Bindu was secretly delighted. But her delight soon turned sour,

for at that very same time, Kapil became dreadfully ill.

The doctors were mystified. Bindu got so worried that she even wrote and told her sister-in-law.

Sumitra replied at once:
I'm dismayed to hear about my beloved brother.
But tell me, Bindu: is the mango tree still flourishing?

Bindu was furious! How could the stupid woman bother about a tree when poor Kapil might be dying? She wrote back, saying exactly that.

The next she knew, Sumitra was on the doorstep.

'I've come to save my brother!' she cried. She rushed past the startled Bindu – not into the sickroom – but out to the garden!

Scarcely catching her breath, she began to water the mango tree, placing huge armfuls of compost around its roots.

By nightfall the tree seemed a little stronger, a little greener.

And in the sickroom, Kapil actually smiled and said he felt quite a bit better.

Day by day, Sumitra nursed

the tree back into life; and day by day Kapil recovered his health.

Within a month, both the mango tree and Kapil were well and strong again; and Sumitra announced that she was returning home.

'Wait!' said Bindu, 'you owe me an explanation. What is your secret? How did you save Kapil's life?'

'Isn't it obvious?' smiled Sumitra. 'When the tree is healthy and happy, so is my brother; but when one falls ill, the other does too, and so on. Now you understand why I was such a careful gardener – for Kapil and the mango tree share the same soul!'

Indian

JOURNEY TO THE LAND OF FLOWERS

Far away lies the Oobi-Oobi Mountain: full of danger, full of magic, for its peak is the pathway to the Sky. No-one has dared to climb it, not for many years, not for countless generations. Ah, but wait, remember . . .

Long, long ago was the Dreamtime. And in its beginning, Baiame the Great One made the world. He created the deserts and rivers, the plants, the animals and all the people.

When he had finished, Baiame strode up Oobi-Oobi and went to his home in the Sky. What a loss! No sooner had he disappeared than the magic he had left behind began to trickle away, down through cracks and gullies to nowhere, leaving the Earth bleak, sad, dry. So his beautiful flowers had nothing left to feed on. One by one, they faded, crumpled up and died.

Soon there were no flowers left anywhere at all. Imagine! No flowers – no colour, no scent. No wonder all the people felt gloomy, heavy hearted.

So a special, secret ceremony was held by the *wirinuns* – the old men, the wise ones, the sorcerers. They painted themselves, they danced and chanted, they called upon their totem, they drew patterns in the bare earth, and they watched for magic signs. Long before night was ended, they had learned what they must do.

In the thin, blue light of dawn the wise men began walking, setting their sights on Oobi-Oobi Mountain. It was a long journey and a hard one, but the old ones had no time to be afraid.

At last they reached the sacred mountain: a vast, bare tower of rock lost in swirling clouds, sheer and smooth, impossible to climb.

Impossible! But the wise men did not give up.

Again they danced and chanted, again they drew their sacred patterns, they waited and they watched.

At last, Baiame heard their prayers and showed them a path, a treacherously jagged slope of crags and footholds carved into the rocks.

The wise men began to climb. It was long and slow, steep and difficult. Through four dawns and four sunsets they struggled on and on, ever upward – until at last they reached the top.

Here, high above the clouds, there was nothing but a bubbling spring of fresh, sweet water and a strange circle of stones. The air was heavy with mysteries. They gazed around. Suddenly a wind stirred, grew into a gale-force roar; and from out of this wind-roar a voice cried:

'Greetings, Earth children! I am Walla-Guroon-Bu-An, messenger to Baiame. The Great One commands me to ask you this: How dare you climb his sacred mountain? Tremble! Then tell me what you want of him.'

Now the wise men were really afraid. They clasped each other and bowed their heads. At last the eldest and cleverest amongst them whispered,

'Forgive us, Walla-Guroon-Bu-An, and may great Baiame forgive us too. We have come here because our people's hearts are broken. All the beauty has gone from the world. We long for flowers!'

Walla-Guroon-Bu-An laughed.

'Come then, you poor, simple creatures. I shall take you to the Sky world. There you will find so many flowers that you . . .'

His last words were swallowed by the wind; the wind became a whirlwind; and then the wise men felt themselves being lifted up by invisible forces into a thick ocean of clouds.

Higher and higher they soared, tossed about and helpless as withered leaves. Then slowly the wind died, and laid them gently to rest on solid ground.

They found themselves in a place that shimmered with colour like a thousand twisted rainbows. There were flowers everywhere! – red, yellow, blue, white, green, violet, orange and every shade between. The air was so thick with their perfumes that the wise men reeled. Clouds of pollen tickled their throats, making them gasp and sneeze. Under their bare, travel-worn feet, the petals were dewy-soft.

'So!' came Walla-Guroon-Bu-An's voice again, 'is this what you dream of? Then take as much as you want from Baiame's garden.

But work quickly, quickly, for the Great One will not let you linger here for long.'

So little time, yet so much to do! At once the wise men set to, bending to pluck enormous armfuls of flowers. Soon they were lost under billowing wreathes of blossoms, yet fast and feverishly still they worked until –

'Stop, stop!' called the messenger's voice.

The wind stirred again: it tossed the flowers above their heads. Before their eyes, the wonderful garden faded into a dim realm of ghosts and the whirlwind of cloud swallowed them up again. Now they were falling, falling, back to the bare stone circle on Oobi-Oobi's peak.

The wise men blinked, leaned together, shook their heads in wonder. Praise be to Baiame, they still had the flowers!

For the last time, Walla-Guroon-Bu-An spoke to them:

'Take these flowers home with you. Give them to your people. Tell them to scatter their seeds far and wide. Baiame's sun and rain will make them grow thickly everywhere: on the trees and shrubs, on the plains and hills, scattered like stars amongst the grass. Sometimes they will fade, as the moon does; but like the moon they will never truly die but always grow strong and bright again. Now go!'

For many weary days the wise men travelled homeward. At last – there were their wives, their sons and daughters, their grandchildren, crowding round to greet them, fingering the dew-soft flowers, breathing in their delicious perfumes, wide-eyed with disbelief.

The wise men told their extraordinary story. Then the people scattered the flower seeds far and wide to the corners of the world, just as Walla-Guroon-Bu-An had commanded them.

Some fell on the tree tops, some on the grass, some on the bare stone and earth; and where each kind landed, there they have grown and bloomed ever since.

All this happened long, long ago; but since that time, it is quite true, the flowers have never, ever died. Our people know that great Baiame will not forget his promise. So even when drought shrivels all things that grow into dry, bony cinders, we do not despair. For our grandfathers tell us, this has happened many times before, yet the flowers will surely come again – for so it has always been since the wise old *wirinuns* brought the blossoms back from the garden in the Sky.

Aboriginal

THE LITTLE PEOPLE AND THE HAWTHORN BUSH

Tim MacDougal's grand-mother had the second sight, and if she told him once, she told him a thousand times:

'The hawthorn is a gentle bush, my boy, for the Little People live deep inside it. So I warn you: don't you go cutting any down, lest you bring about some dreadful revenge!'

'Old wives' tales!' guffawed Tim; but he remembered her stories, just the same.

Well, Grandmother died and Tim got married, and soon his wife had a lovely baby son. Only one thing spoiled their happiness: there was never enough money to go round.

So when he heard of a local farmer offering a fat payment if someone would chop down some bushes that were spoiling his

pasture, Tim was quick to offer himself for the job.

The two shook hands on it. Then Tim asked, 'What bushes are they, anyway?'

'Hawthorn,' said the farmer shortly.

Tim paled and he tried not to think of Grandmother's warnings. He needed that money really badly; besides, he couldn't go back on a deal.

So next morning, he set off with his axe. The farmer met him in the pasture, showed him the hawthorns that wanted felling, and slapped a pile of coins into his hand. Then he hurried away, leaving Tim to get on with the task.

Phut! Phut! Phut! His axe sliced through the gnarled old trunks and the little bushes tumbled to the ground.

Tim glanced nervously over his shoulder; but he caught neither sight nor sound of the fairy folk.

As soon as he was finished, and the bushes all neatly piled up, he jingled the new coins in his pocket and hurried home.

There, what should he find but his wife weeping great rivers of tears.

'The baby's gone!' she sobbed. 'I just popped out for a moment – and when I came back the cot was empty!'

'Oh no! It's the revenge of the fairies after all!' exclaimed Tim. He was almost sobbing himself as he confessed his foolhardy deed.

'Why, you careless, money-grabbing idiot!' screamed his wife. Then, seizing their meagre handful of savings all for herself, she went

storming out of the house.

Tim was in a frantic panic: there was no time to lose! In a daze, he hunted out the old book of magic charms that his grandmother had left to him. He pored over the dusty pages until he found the very remedy he needed:

Of Hawthornes and the Pleasinge of Faeries that Dwelle Thereinne . . .

Quick as he could, he memorised the curious instructions. Then he raced back to the pasture where the fallen bushes still lay.

With trembling fingers, Tim broke off all the twigs that carried buds and carried them carefully across to a clump of wild thyme. There he poked them into the earth, forming a neat circle of hawthorn twigs around the sweet smelling herb.

Then he crossed his fingers for luck and slunk off home to wait through the night.

At dawn he rushed back – and oh joy, some magic had surely happened ! For the hawthorn shoots had grown into a thicket of wind-twisted bushes! Moreover, from

deep in their midst came the quavering of a familiar baby's cry.

Tim pushed and fought his way through the scratchy bushes. There, safe and well (though rather cross and hungry!) was his own dear, tiny son.

As for his wife – well, the fairies sent her marching home too; for doesn't every wee child want its mother?

Now then! Who knows which bushes the fairies might lurk in? So you'd better heed this tale as well as you've heard it – and don't go scoffing at the old folks' wisdom!

Irish

THE BAMBOO PRINCESS

There was once a young man called Khatib Malim Seleman who walked by the edge of the jungle. Suddenly he gave a gasp of wonder. Fleeing from the sunlight into the thickets where mist veiled the twisted leaves, he caught sight of a beautiful ghost!

Her long black hair was hung with shimmering pearls and jewels. Her flowing silken robes were fine as gossamer. What could she be? The ghost of a princess!

'I must follow her!' he exclaimed – for that one sight had made him mad with love. Pushing aside the first trees and creepers, he went after her shadow into the jungle's depths.

He hurried and stumbled over roots and snakes, alone with the chattering of monkeys and the shrieking of coloured birds. Sometimes he thought he saw her again: then his heart raced and his pace quickened – but never enough to catch her up.

Soon night fell. Through the hot, green darkness, Khatib Malim Seleman wandered on until he came to a clearing. He was utterly worn out. Sinking to the ground, he fell at once into a deep sleep.

He dreamed that he was surrounded by tall, gracefully arched bamboos. Through their stems walked the ghost-girl, carrying plates piled high with delicious food.

'Let us eat together,' she invited him.

So they sat side by side in the bamboo grove, feasting, laughing and talking together all through the night.

It seemed that Khatib Malim Seleman's quest was almost ended. He knelt before the princess and asked her to marry him.

'*No*!' Her cry was frightened and shrill. 'Look: beyond the stems the sun is rising! That means I must leave you for ever . . . unless . . . unless . . .'

'Wait! Where are you going to?' Wild with anguish, Khatib Malim Seleman tried to stop her –

But even as her words faded, the lovely girl was fading too.

'Princess! Come back! You must at least . . . Tell me how I can find you again!'

'So near! So far! I am locked away . . . Inside the bamboo – oo – oo . . .'

★

Khatib Malim Seleman sat up, opened his eyes, blinked. Had he really been asleep? And yet – how strange: overnight, bamboo stems had miraculously sprung up and filled the clearing where he lay. Could it be that his lost princess was really trapped inside one?

The ghost girl's last words echoed inside his head. He must find her!

He drew the knife from his belt and pulled the nearest stem towards him.

Slowly, gently, he sliced the knife down through it. He must take care: for if the princess *were* inside – oh, it was unthinkable that he might hurt her!

Time stood still: the whole jungle held its breath.

His knife reached the bottom. The two halves of split bamboo fell apart, like hollow fragments of broken eggshell, and –

Out stepped the princess!

She tossed her long black hair and smiled at him.

'At last! How wonderful to be free! Who knows how long I have wept and waited inside that terrible enchanted prison! Oh my noble rescuer, I beg you, follow me once more, for our fate is surely to find paradise together!'

So hand in hand they wandered, as far as distant Bukit Peraja; and there they disappeared for ever.

They live there still. It is said that the Bamboo Princess is so happy now, that she loves to perform kind deeds for anyone who asks it.

If ever you need her help, go to the bamboo groves and call on her there.

May she come, may she do what she can for you! Ah, then like a dream she will vanish away into the mist.

Malay

THE CORN MAIDEN

Long ago when the world was young, the people were often hungry. They survived as best they could by hunting animals and gathering wild fruits. There were no farmers and no-one knew how to grow corn. Without corn there was no flour, and without flour there was no bread to eat.

At that time there lived an old, old woman who understood many things. One day she called together all her family, all her neighbours and told them:

'Something wonderful is coming! For ten nights I have heard it singing from the river. Now it is time for you to listen with me, for we must find out who or what it is.'

So when darkness fell, the whole village went down to the river bank. Soon they heard a voice as sweet as a summer wind quivering over the water:

'Fair and fine,
Fine and fair
Are the fields
Where I grow and ripen.'

The villagers peered and strained to see who it was that sang so hauntingly. But they could see nothing, no-one.

Yet trusting in the Great Spirit, they sang back their own chant of peace and welcome.

The strange singing swelled to fill the darkness, until it seemed that a great army of mysteries was washing towards them through the night. Then the youngest children began to whimper with fear.

'Don't worry,' the old, old woman told them. 'You can go home now. Take your mothers and fathers with you. Leave me here. I am not afraid. I shall meet the singer and find out what I must do.'

So the villagers went away and the old, old woman waited, bent and wrinkled, alone.

Many moments of stillness passed; then suddenly the singer called out,

'Grandmother! Bring me ashore!'

'I am coming my child,' replied the old, old woman.

She climbed into her canoe and paddled it out to the centre of the river. There she saw an enormous beaver. His back was arched out of the water, and on it sat a graceful girl.

The girl jumped into the canoe, and the old, old woman rowed her ashore.

'Thank you Grandmother,' said she. 'Now you must leave me here and go home yourself. But be sure to come and look for me in the morning.'

The old, old woman did as she was bidden. The next day, as soon as dawn had washed the sky, she hurried back to the river bank.

There was no-one there; but a single stalk of corn, thick with golden seed, was growing on the spot where the mysterious singer had landed.

The old, old woman smiled and nodded to herself. She plucked the corn and carried it carefully home to her wigwam. There she hung it on a pole by her fireplace and waited to see what would

happen next.

That night she had a dream. In it, the corn changed back into the shape of the girl she had rescued.

'Grandmother,' she said, 'it is too hot for me by your fire. Take me outside, I beg you! Then plant my seeds in the ground.'

When she woke, the old, old woman remembered her dream at once. Carefully, she unhooked the corn stalk and shook out the grains into a bowl. Then she carried them outside, laid them in the ground and covered them with a soft sprinkling of soil.

The sun shone and the rain fell. Soon green shoots pushed through the blanket of earth.

Then the old, old woman had another dream about the girl.

'Grandmother,' said she, 'know this: I am Corn. I have come to feed you. Nurse me carefully, protect me from the weeds. When I am ripe, grind me into flour. When that is done, bake me into bread. Eat me. Share me generously with your people. I will make you all strong!'

Once again, the old, old woman did as she was bidden. She looked after the corn. Moons waxed and waned, summer blossomed and faded. The corn grew strong. Its seed ripened.

It was the time of leaf-fall. The old, old woman harvested the corn. She divided it up and gave a handful of seeds to every family in the village.

Then she shared with them the wisdom that the Corn Maiden had taught her.

That night, everyone was happy. Now they had delicious bread to eat. Never again would they be hungry!

They went down to the river bank and chanted their thanks to the Corn Maiden.

For the last time they heard her singing across the water, but now her words were tinged with a strange sadness:

'Take care, take care
Of the good Earth that feeds me!
I am the fruit of the Earth –
Oh I suffer!
Do not waste me,
*   do not poison me . . .'*

'Whatever can it mean?' asked the villagers.

Tears ran down the old, old woman's cheeks, for she could see far into the future.

'Corn is sacred, everything that grows is sacred,' she said. 'But I warn you, there will come a time when the sons of your sons will forget this. Then hunger and sorrow will return to the world.'

She shook her head. 'It will not end until – *unless* – their grandchildren learn once more this lesson – the only lesson that is worth remembering: how to love and respect the Earth.'

Iroquois Indian